teacher's friend publications

CLIP ART for Autumn

thematic, reproducible illustrations for the classroom by karen sevaly

...use for student papers, worksheets, newsletters, nametags, awards, parent notes, mobiles, calendars and much, much more!!!

(These illustrations have been previously published by Teacher's Friend.)

This book is dedicated
to
teachers and children
everywhere!

Printed in the United States of America.
Published by Teacher's Friend Publications, Inc.
7407 Orangewood Drive, Riverside, CA 92504

ISBN 0-943263-45-X

Making the Most of it!

Save Your Clip Art Book! Photocopy and File for Future Use.

CLIP ART

The illustrations on these pages may be used in classroom bulletins, newspapers, notes home or just to decorate your own worksheets. Simply photocopy the illustrations, cut them out and paste them to your originals before printing. The drawings may be enlarged or reduced on some copy machines. You are also free to enlarge the characters for other uses, such as: bulletin boards, calendar decorations, booklet covers and awards.

HOW TO USE THIS BOOK:

Every page of this book may be duplicated for individual classroom use.

Some pages may be copied onto construction paper or tagboard for durability or used as they are.

If you have access to a print shop, you will find that many pages work well when printed on index paper. This type of paper takes crayons and felt markers well and is sturdy enough to last and last.

Lastly, some pages are meant to be enlarged with an overhead or opaque projector. When we say enlarge, we mean it! Think BIG! Three, four, or even five feet is great! Try using colored butcher paper or poster board so you don't spend all your time coloring.

BULLETIN BOARDS:

Creating clever bulletin boards for your classroom need not take fantastic amounts of time and money. With a little preparation and know-how you can have different boards each month with very little effort. Try some of these ideas:

1. Background paper should be put up only once a year. Choose colors that can go with many themes and holidays. A black butcher paper background will look terrific with springtime butterflies or a spooky Halloween display.
2. Butcher paper is not the only thing that can be used to cover the back of your board. You might like to try the classified ad section of the local newspaper for a current events board. Or how about colored burlap? Just fold it up at the end of the year to reuse again.
3. Wall paper is another great background cover. Discontinued rolls can be purchased for next to nothing at discount hardware stores. Most can be wiped clean and will not fade like construction paper. (Do not glue wallpaper directly to the board, just staple or pin in place.)

Making the Most of it!

ON-GOING BULLETIN BOARDS:

Creating on-going bulletin board can be easy. Give one of these ideas a try.

1. Choose one board to be a calendar display. Students can change this monthly. They can do the switching of dates, month titles and holiday symbols. Start the year with a great calendar board and with a few minor changes each month it will add a sparkle to the classroom.

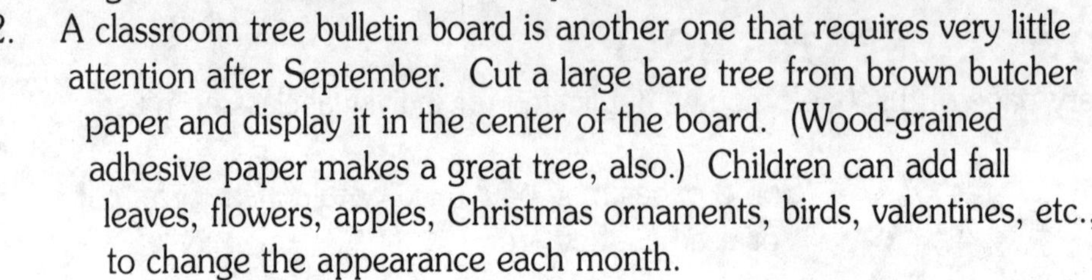

2. A classroom tree bulletin board is another one that requires very little attention after September. Cut a large bare tree from brown butcher paper and display it in the center of the board. (Wood-grained adhesive paper makes a great tree, also.) Children can add fall leaves, flowers, apples, Christmas ornaments, birds, valentines, etc., to change the appearance each month.
3. Birthday bulletin boards, classroom helpers, school announcement displays and reading group charts can all be created once before school starts and changed monthly with very little effort. With all these on-going ideas, you'll discover that all that bulletin board space seems smaller than you thought.

MOBILES:

Making mobiles are especially fun for all ages. Teachers may like to simplify mobile construction for younger children by using one of these ideas.

DRINKING STRAW MOBILE - Thread a piece of yarn through a plastic drinking straw and tie a mobile pattern to each end. Flatten a paper clip and bend it around the center of the straw for hanging. The mobile can easily be balanced by adjusting the yarn. (Older students can make their mobiles the same way but may wish to add additional levels by hanging other mobiles directly below the first.)

CLOTHES HANGER MOBILE - Mobiles can easily be made with a wire clothes hanger, as shown. Just tie each pattern piece to the hanger with thread, yarn or kite string.

YARN MOBILE - The most simple mobile is made by gluing the pattern pieces to a length of yarn, each piece spaced directly beneath the other. Tie a bow at the top and hang in a window or from the ceiling.

Making the Most of it!

CLASSROOM HELPERS

CLASSROOM HELPERS

LETTERING AND HEADINGS:

Not every school has a letter machine that produces perfect 2" or 4" letters from construction paper. (There is such a thing, you know.) The rest of us will just have to use the old stencil and scissor method. But wait, there is an easier way!

1. Don't cut individual letters. They are difficult to pin up straight, anyway. Instead, hand print bulletin board titles and headings onto strips of colored paper. When it is time for the board to come down, simply roll it up to use again next year.

   Use your imagination. Try cloud shapes and cartoon bubbles. They will all look great.

2. Hand lettering is not that difficult, even if your printing is not up to penmanship standards. Print block letters with a felt marker. Draw big dots at the ends of each letter. This will hide any mistakes and add a charming touch to the overall effect.

ADDING THE COLOR:

Putting the color to finished items can be a real bother to teachers in a rush. Try these ideas:

1. On small areas, water color markers work great. If your area is rather large switch to crayons or even colored chalk or pastels. (Don't worry, lamination or a spray fixative will keep the color on the work and off of you. No laminator or fixative? That's okay, a little hair spray will do the trick.)
2. The quickest method of coloring large items is to simply start with colored paper. (Poster board, butcher paper and large construction paper work well.) Add a few dashes of a contrasting colored marker or crayon and you will have it made.
3. Try cutting character eyes, teeth, etc. from white typing paper and gluing them in place. These features will really stand out and make your bulletin boards come alive.
   For special effects add real buttons or lace. Metallic paper looks great on stars and belt buckles, too.

Making the Most of it!

LAMINATORS:

If you have access to a roll laminator you already know how fortunate you are. They are priceless when it comes to saving time and money. Try these ideas:

1. You can laminate more than just classroom posters and construction paper. Try various kinds of fabric, wall paper and gift wrapping. You'll be surprised at the great combinations you come up with.

Laminated classified ads can be used to cut headings for current event bulletin boards. Colorful gingham fabric makes terrific cut letters or scalloped edging. You might even try burlap! It looks terrific on a fall bulletin board.

(You can even make professional looking bookmarks with laminated fabric or burlap. They are great gift ideas.)

2. Felt markers and laminated paper or fabric can work as a team. Just make sure the markers you use are permanent and not water based. Oops, make a mistake! That's okay. Put a little lighter fluid on a tissue, rub across the mark and presto, it's gone! (Dry transfer markers work great on lamination, too.)
3. Laminating cut-out characters can be tricky. If you have enlarged an illustration onto poster board, simply laminate first and then cut it out with an art knife. (Just make sure the laminator is plenty hot.)

One problem may arise when you paste an illustration onto poster board and laminate the finished product. If your paste-up does not cover 100% of the illustration, the poster board may separate from it after laminating. To avoid this problem, paste your illustration onto poster board that measures slightly larger. This way, the lamination will help hold down your illustration.

Have you ever laminated student-made place mats, crayon shavings, tissue paper collages, or dried flowers? You'll be amazed at the variety of creative things that can be laminated and used in the classroom, or as take-home gifts.

AUTUMN

Harvest

September
SEPTEMBER

September

Start of School

September
#1 GRAND-PARENT
OUR SEPTEMBER NEWSLETTER

Homework!
Spelling!

My
Grandmother
My
Grandfather

Apple
Seeds
Apple
Time

SUPER!

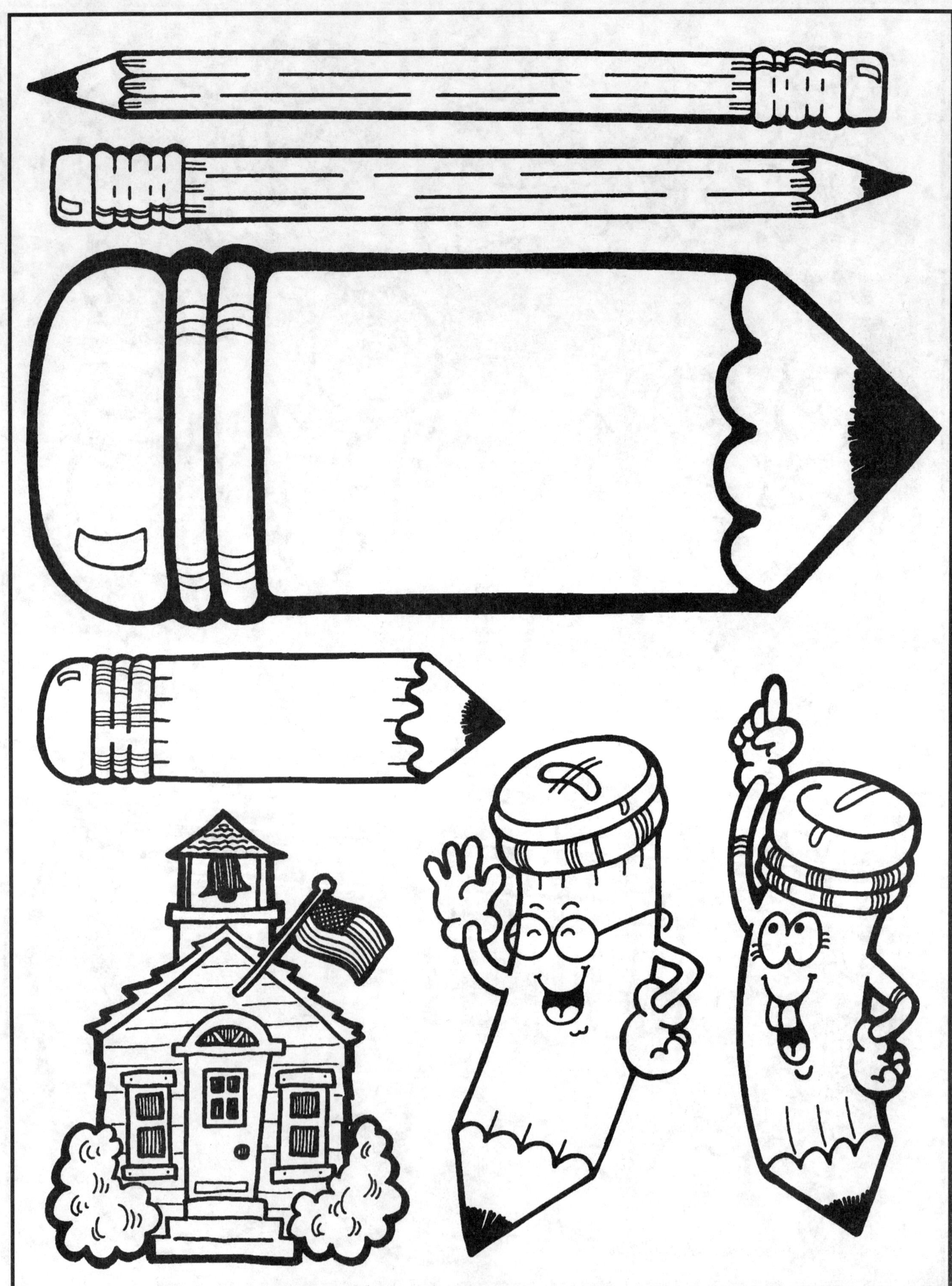

October
October
"TRICK OR TREAT"

October
OCTOBER

HALLOWEEN
TRICK or Treat

Halloween
TRICK OR TREAT

Whoooo
Knows?

BOO!
"Hi!"

WOW!

Fire Safety
FD
5
5
5

Dinosaurs

FOOTBALL
12

GO!
13

November

November
NOVEMBER

November
OUR
NOVEMBER
NEWSLETTER

Children's
Book
Week

DICTIONARY
ALMANAC

THANKSGIVING

Pilgrims and Indians

GREAT!

Election Day
VOTE!
VOTE
President
Vice-President
USA